D0712919

DIARY OF
CARRIE BERRY
A
CONFEDERATE GIRL

by Carrie Berry

CAPSTONE PRESS
a capstone imprint

Fact Finders are published by Capstone Press,
1710 Roe Crest Drive, North Mankato, Minnesota 56003
www.capstonepub.com

Library of Congress Cataloging-in-Publication Data
Berry, Carrie, 1854–1921.
  Diary of Carrie Berry : a Confederate girl / by Carrie Berry.
    pages cm.—(Fact finders. First-person histories)
  Summary: "Presents excerpts from the diary of Carrie Berry, a 10-year-old girl who lived in the
Confederate South in 1864"—Provided by publisher.
  Includes bibliographical references and index.
ISBN 978-1-4765-4192-1 (library binding)—ISBN 978-1-4765-5135-7 (paperback)—
ISBN 978-1-4765-5984-1 (ebook pdf)
1. Berry, Carrie, 1854–1921—Diaries—Juvenile literature. 2. Girls—Georgia—Atlanta—Diaries—
Juvenile literature. 3. United States—History—Civil War, 1861–1865—Personal narratives,
Confederate—Juvenile literature. 4. Atlanta (Ga.)—Biography—Juvenile literature. 5. Atlanta (Ga.)—
History, Military—19th century—Juvenile literature. 6. Atlanta (Ga.)—Social life and customs—19th
century—Juvenile literature. 7. United States—History—Civil War, 1861-1865—Social aspects—
Juvenile literature. I. Title.
  E605.B52 2014
  973.7'82092—dc23 [B]   2013035324

Editorial Credits
Erika L. Shores, editor; Bobbie Nuytten, designer; Wanda Winch, media researcher; Laura Manthe,
production specialist

Photo Credits
Atlanta History Center: Kenan Research Center, cover (portrait left), 5; Corbis, 13; CriaImages.com:
Jay Robert Nash Collection, 16; Getty Images Inc: Buyenlarge, 22–23; Library of Congress: Prints and
Photographs Division, cover (right), 1, 7, 8, 10, 15, 19 (left), 21, 24, 26, 28, 29 (all); Shutterstock: Andrzej
Sowa, cover (l), ayzek, (flag), B. Calkins, 20, Becky Stares, 12, Brittny, 25, Katya Ulitina, cover (back),
Mediagram, 6, Picsfive (ripped paper element), Seregam, 19 (right)

Editor's Note
This book contains only portions of Carrie Berry's diary. Carrie Berry's original diary is currently held
at the Atlanta History Center in Atlanta, Georgia.

Printed in the United States of America in Stevens Point, Wisconsin.
092013   007769WZS14

TABLE OF CONTENTS

A Confederate Girl

Carrie Berry was like any other 10-year-old southern girl in the 1860s. She did schoolwork, had chores to do, and fought with her siblings. But in 1864 Carrie's life changed forever. Carrie and her family lived in Atlanta, Georgia. They were Confederates, which means they believed states should decide their laws, including whether slavery should be allowed. By the 1860s slavery had long been part of the way of life in the Southern states. Southern **plantations** grew much of the world's cotton and sugarcane. Plantation owners used slaves to grow and pick the crops.

Northerners said slavery should be the federal government's business. Slavery was illegal in the North. When Abraham Lincoln ran for president in 1860, he promised that slavery would not be allowed in any new states or **territories**. When Lincoln won the election, Southerners believed their way of life was being threatened. By February 1861, 11 Southern states had left the Union and formed a new country called the Confederate States of America. By April the Northern Union states and the Southern Confederate states were at war.

Most Civil War battles were fought in the Confederate states. Southern cities such as Atlanta, where Carrie lived, were heavily damaged. From May to September 1864, Confederate troops tried to keep the Union Army from taking over Atlanta.

On September 1, 1864, Union General William Tecumseh Sherman and his troops won the battle for Atlanta. On November 15, Sherman had his troops burn the city. Sherman then marched his army of 68,000 soldiers from Atlanta to Savannah, Georgia. The troops burned buildings and homes along the way. They took every bit of food they could find.

Carrie kept a diary during the many battles fought in and around Atlanta. She wrote about her experiences and feelings. She tells what life was like for a Confederate girl during the Civil War.

Carrie Berry as a teenager

plantation—a large farm where crops such as cotton and sugarcane are grown; before 1865, plantations were run by slave labor

territory—an area under the control of a country

5

THE Diary OF Carrie Berry, 1864

Aug. 3. Wednesday—

this was my birthday. I was ten years old, But I did not have a cake times were too hard so I celebrated with ironing. I hope by my next birthday we will have peace in our land so that I can have a nice dinner.

Aug. 4. Thurs.—

The shells have ben flying all day and we have stayed in the cellar. Mama put me on [knitting] some stockings this morning and I will try to finish them before school **commences**. I knit all the morning. In the evening we had to run to Auntie's and get in the cellar. We did not feel safe in our cellar, they [the shells] fell so thick and fast.

Carrie's diary entries appear word for word as they were written, whenever possible. Because the diary appears in its original form, you will notice misspellings and mistakes in grammar. To make Carrie's meaning clear, in some instances, corrections or explanations within a set of brackets sometimes follow the mistakes.

Shells were large iron containers filled with black powder. Soldiers fired these shells from cannons. The shells exploded when they landed on the ground. Soldiers could fire shells from far away, but the shells did not always accurately hit their targets.

Aug. 9. Tues.—

We have had to stay in the cellar all day the shells have ben falling so thick around the house. Two have fallen in the garden, but none of us were hurt. Cousin Henry Beatty came in a and wanted us to move, he thought that we were in danger, but we will try it [here] a little longer.

Union General William T. Sherman and his army arrived outside the city of Atlanta by the middle of July 1864. For the next two months, the Union Army continued to battle Confederate troops around the city.

In 1864 Confederate troops built forts to defend Atlanta against Union attacks.

commence—to begin or start

Aug. 15. Mon.—

We had no shells this morning when we got up and we thought that we would not have any to day (but, my, when will they stop) but soon after breakfast Zuie and I were standing on the platform between the house and the dining room. It made a very large hole in the garden and threw the dirt all over the yard. I never was so frightened in my life. Zuie was as pale as a **corpse** and I expect I was too. It did not take us long to fly to the cellar. We stayed out till night though we had them all day but they did not come so near us again.

Zuie was Carrie's sister. Her other siblings were Fannie, Maggie, and Maxwell.

General Sherman, leaning on gun at right, and Union troops at Federal Fort No. 7 in 1864

Aug. 16. Tues.—

We had shells all night. There was a large piece came through Mama's room directly after we went to bed and fell on the little bed and I expect if we had been sleeping there some of us would have ben hurt. Cousin Henry and Cousin Eddy came to see us to day. They told us that they did not think the Federals would be here much longer to **torment** us and I hope that it may be so for we are getting very tired of living so.

People loyal to the United States government were called Federals by Southerners.

August 18. Thurs.—

When I woke this morning I thought the hole [whole] town would be torn up. The cannons were so near and so loud but we soon found out that it was our guns so we have ben very well content all day. We have had less shells to day tan [than] we have had in a week.

Aug. 21. Sun.—

This was a dark rainy morning and we thought we would have a quiet Sunday but we were disappointed. Papa says that we will have to move down town some where. Our cellar is not safe.

corpse—a dead body

torment—to cause pain and suffering

Aug. 23 Tues. —

We feel very comfortable since we have moved but Mama is **fretted** to death all the time for fear of fire. There is a fire in town nearly every day. I get so tired of being housed up all the time. The shells get worse and worse every day. O that something would stop them.

Aug. 26. Fri. —

Cousin Henry came in this morning and told us we need not fear the shells any more. The Yankess left there [their] brest works [breastworks] and he hoped they were on the way back to Tennessee. We have had such a delightful day. We all wanted to move to day but we will wait til to morrow and see if the Yankees have gone.

Breastworks were barriers built by soldiers to protect them from enemy gunfire.

Confederate soldiers placed barriers throughout Atlanta in 1864 in an effort to keep out Union troops.

The Blue and Gray War

The Civil War is sometimes called the Blue and Gray War. Soldiers who fought for the North wore blue uniforms. These soldiers were called Federals, Northerners, Union soldiers, or Yankees. Soldiers who fought for the South were called Confederates, Southerners, Rebels, or Johnny Rebs. Confederate soldiers wore gray uniforms.

Confederate soldiers could not always wear gray uniforms in the later years of the Civil War. In 1863 a Northern **blockade** kept supplies from reaching the South. The Confederates could not get the dye needed to make uniforms gray. Instead, they ground up walnut shells to make a dye. But the walnut shells gave the uniforms a brown color called butternut. This color led people to give Confederate soldiers the name butternuts.

fret—to worry constantly

blockade—a closing off of an area to keep people or supplies from going in or out

11

Aug. 27. Sat.—

We moved home this morning and we have ben buisy trying to get things **regulated**. I feel so glad to get home and have no shells around us.

Aug. 30. Tues.—

Miss Fannie Homes came around this morning to see about her school. I was so glad to see my old teacher once more. I hope she will commence her school. I am tired of staying at home.

In the 1860s few states provided public education. Teachers often ran their own schools and taught several grades in one room.

Thousands of citizens were forced to evacuate to areas north or south of Atlanta.

Sept. 1. Thurs. —

We did not get home untill twelve o'clock. We had a very pleasant time and every thing seemed quiet. Directly after dinner Cousin Emma came down and told us that Atlanta would be **evacuated** this evening and we might look for the federals in the morning. It was not long till the hole [whole] town found it out and such excitement there was. We have ben looking for them all the evening but they have not come yet …

regulate—to arrange or order
evacuate—to leave an area during a time of danger

Sept. 2. Fri.—

We all woke up this morning without sleeping much last night. The Confederates had four engenes [engines] and a long train of box cars filled with amunition **[ammunition]** and set it on fire last night which caused a grate [great] explosion which kept us all awake. Every one has been trying to get all they could before the Federals come in the morning. They have ben running with saques [sacks] of meal, salt and tobacco. They did act rediculous breaking open stores and robbing them. About twelve o'clock there were a few federals came in. They were all frightened. We were afraid they were going to treat us badly. It was not long till the Infantry came in. They were orderely and behaved very well. I think I shall like the Yankees very well.

After months of fighting, Sherman and the Union Army captured Atlanta on September 1, 1864. The next day Sherman marched into the city. He turned Atlanta into a large Union Army camp and ordered all the citizens of Atlanta to leave.

Sun. Sept. 4.—

Another long and lonesome Sunday. How I wish we could have Church and Sunday School. We have ben looking at the soldiers all day. They have come in by the thousand. They were playing bands and they seemed to be rejoiced. It has not seemed like Sunday.

Drums and brass bands played an important role in Civil War armies. Soldiers marched to the music. Band concerts entertained the troops at night.

ammunition—bullets and other objects that can be fired from weapons

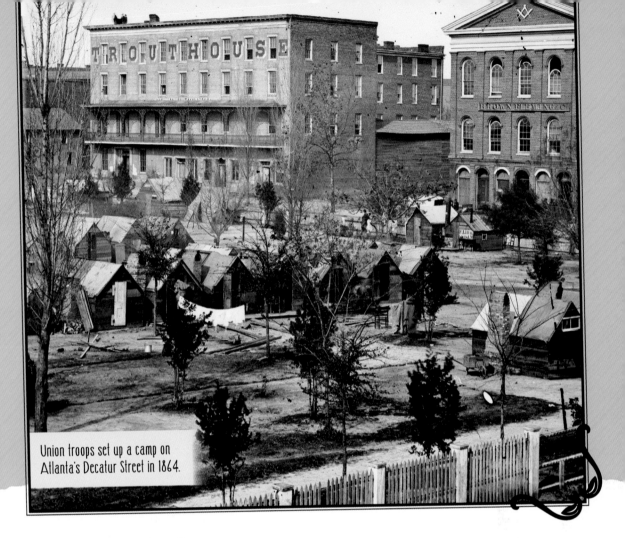

Union troops set up a camp on Atlanta's Decatur Street in 1864.

Thurs. Sept. 8. —

We all went to wirk [work] in glad spirits this morning. Me and Tilo went to ironing. Mama was buisy regulating things when Papa came and told us that Gen. Sherman had ordered us to move. It broke all into our rangements [arrangements].

Fri. Sept. 9. —

We all comenced this morning to prepare for moving. We don't know how long we will get to stay here. We are all in so much trouble.

Evacuating citizens had to pack their belongings and find temporary places to live.

Sat. Sept. 10.—

Every one I see seems sad. The citizens all think that it is the most cruel thing to drive us from our home but I think it would be so funny to move. Mama seems so troubled and she can't do any thing. Papa says he don't know where on earth to go.

Mon. Sept. 12.—

We commenced packing up to move. We did not do much. Papa herd [heard] up town there was a chance for us to stay if he could get into business.

Many children played with rag dolls during the Civil War. Rag dolls were easy to make from scraps of old clothes and other household items. Children spent many hours making handmade clothes for their rag dolls.

Tues. Sept. 13.—

Papa got into business to day and the rest of us went to wirk in good **earnest** thinking that we will get to stay. I hope that we will get to stay. Mama dislikes to move so much.

Mon. Sept. 19.—

I went over to Aunt Healy this morning. She is packing up to move and I feel sorry that she is going away. We will miss her so much.

Tues. Sept. 27.—

This has been wash day. I went up to Aunties this evening and she gave me some quilt peaces [pieces] and some doll clothes.

Sun. Oct. 2.—

This has ben a very pretty day. I went around to Mrs. Lesters. Ella and I took a walk to see how the soldiers had torn down the fine houses. It is a shame to see the fine houses torn down.

earnest—serious

Mon. Oct. 3. —

We herd [heard] that General Hood had to go away around towards Chattanooga [Tennessee] tearing up the railroad. The federals seemed very much trouble about it. I commenced Sister a little **worsted** dress. I love to sew for her because she loves me.

Confederate Army General John Hood damaged his army's own railroads. The Confederates did not want the Union Army to use them. Railroads were important during the Civil War. Both sides relied on trains to deliver supplies such as weapons and food to their armies.

Wed. Oct. 5. —

...I went up to Aunties and she was selling out to go north. She is afraid that Gen. Hood will get back and commence shelling as the federals did. I don't blame her for I never would stay and be shelled again if I could get away, though we will be very sorry when she leaves.

Sun. Oct. 23. —

This has ben a beautiful day since the sun has come out. Mama and Papa took a walk this evening and they say that they never saw a place torn up like Atlanta is. Half of the houses are torn down.

Tues. Nov. 8. —

This is Zuie's birthday and she has [to] be very smart [look neat and tidy]. We lost our last hog this morning early. Soldiers took him out of the pen. Me and Buddie went around to hunt for him and everywhere that we inquired they would say that they saw two soldiers driving off to kill him. We will have to live on bread.

worsted—a smooth type of yarn

An illustration from an 1863 newspaper shows people in the South demanding fair food prices.

Bread Riots

Bread riots were common in the South during the Civil War because food was scarce. The Confederate government sold much of the food to the Confederate Army for the soldiers. Citizens had to pay a higher price for food than the army did. Many families could not afford to buy bread and other necessities. Citizens often went hungry.

Hunger sometimes drove people to march into a store and demand food at army prices. If the store owners refused, angry citizens stole the food.

Fri. Nov. 11.—

This is the last day that cars [passenger trains] are going out to Chattanooga. We are erbliged **[obliged]** to stay here now. Aunt Marthy went down to the carshed [station] and I expect that she got off as she has not ben back.

Sat. Nov. 12.—

We were fritened [frightened] almost to death last night. Some mean soldiers set several houses on fire in different parts of the town. I could not go to sleep for fear that they would set our house on fire. ...

Sherman gave orders to burn all the factories, mills, railroads, and warehouses in Atlanta before his troops left the city. Flames from these fires spread to neighboring homes. Some Union soldiers set fires on their own. They destroyed many private homes.

Tues. Nov 15.—

This has ben a dreadful day. Things have ben burning all around us. We dread to night because we do not know what moment that they will set our house on fire. We have had a gard [guard] a little while after dinner and we feel a little more protected.

oblige—to feel forced to do something

In November 1864 Sherman's troops destroyed Atlanta's railroad depot and other important buildings so Southerners could not rebuild quickly.

Sherman's March

Union General William T. Sherman and his troops captured Atlanta, Georgia, on September 1, 1864. Sherman kept his men in Atlanta to keep the Confederate Army from recapturing it. But by November, the Confederates had been defeated in a number of battles and had lost many soldiers. The Union no longer feared losing Atlanta.

Sherman decided to destroy the Confederate Army by leaving Atlanta and marching his troops eastward toward the sea.

On their march toward the Atlantic Ocean, the Union Army destroyed an area of the Confederacy more than 50 miles (80 kilometers) wide and 300 miles (483 km) long. The army divided into two groups. On December 10, one army group reached Savannah, Georgia, and captured the city. On February 17, 1865, the other army group captured Columbia, South Carolina.

Wed. Nov. 16. —

Oh what a night we had. They came burning the store house and about night it looked like the whole town was on fire. We all set up all night. If we had not set up our house would have ben burnt up for the fire was very near and the soldiers were going around setting houses on fire where they were not watched. They behaved very badly. They all left the town about one o'clock this evening and we were glad when they left for no body know what we have suffered since they came in.

Union troops burned Atlanta's railroad roundhouse. Roundhouses were used to repair locomotives.

Thurs. Nov. 17.—

Everything was so quiet we were afraid that the yankees will come back and finish burning the houses but they did not. They have left. Some Confederates came in here to day and the town is full of country people seeing what they can find. We have ben picking up some things.

Sun. Nov. 27.—

This has ben a beautiful day and everything seems so quiet. There have ben a grate [great] many cittizens [citizens] coming back.

When General Sherman's troops left Atlanta, many of the city's citizens returned. They came home to burned buildings and houses. Those people who found their houses still standing often were shocked to find their possessions stolen or destroyed.

General Sherman's troops photographed in 1864 tearing up railroad tracks at Atlanta's depot.

Wed. Nov. 30. —

We have ben resting to day. The cittizens are still coming in and it wont be very long untill they get the railroad fixed up from here to Macon [Georgia] and then I hope I can see Grandma.

Wed. Dec. 7. —

This has ben a election day for Mayor and council men but the election was broken up. I had a little sister [Mama had a new baby] this morning at eight o'clock and Mama gave her to me [to hold]. I think [the baby is] very pretty. I had to cook breakfast and dinner and supper.

Fri. Dec. 9.—

I made up some buiskets [biscuits] last night and Mama says they were nice. Every moment I can get I am making things to do on the [Christmas] tree. Ella and I are going to have one together. This has ben a cold sleaty [sleety] day.

Tues. Dec. 13.—

... I have made Papa some buesket [biscuits] and pies to take with him to Macon. He is going to try to get in business.

Wed. Dec. 14.—

Papa started to Macon [Georgia] this morning. Mama and me have ben buisy making Fannie and Zuie a rag doll. We feel very lonesome with Papa so far away and the weather is so bad we cant get out.

Mon. Dec. 19.—

It has ben pleasant to day. Ella came to stay all night with me and just as we were going to supper Papa came in and such joy as we all had.

Citizens returning in November 1864 found buildings either destroyed or robbed of all their contents.

Citizens who were away from Atlanta during the shelling and the burning were not prepared for the wreckage. They were angry with Union soldiers for destroying their homes and their city. Some citizens blamed the Southerners who had not left Atlanta during the battle. They did not understand why those who stayed did not stop the Union soldiers from burning the city.

Wed. Dec. 21.—

Papa has to go back to Macon next week and we fear he will be put in servis [military service]. He has ben buisy all day making me a pair of shoes. I do hope he will get off. the people are treating the citizens so **mean** that stayed here with the yankees.

Sat. Dec. 24.—

I have been buisy to day making cakes to **trim** the tree and Ella and I have it all ready trimed and we are all going to night to see it. I think it looks very pretty. We will be sorry when it is all over.

Sun. Dec. 25, 1864.—

We all went down last night to see the tree and how pretty it looked. The room was full of ladies and children and Cap. gave us music on the pianno and tried to do all he could to make us enjoy our selves and we did have a merry time. All came home perfectly satisfied. This has ben a cold dark day but we all went down to see how the tree looked in the day time but it was not as pretty as at night.

Mon. Dec. 26.—

Papa left us this morning. He has gone to Macon to be tried for staying here with the yankees. We are afraid they will put him in the army. We are very sad.

Tues. Dec. 28.—

Some little girls came up here last night and we had a concert and enjoyed our selves very much. At one o'clock we let the tree fall and then came home and had a party. Now our Christmas ended with a hail storm.

trim—decorate

About Carrie's Life

Carrie lived in Atlanta her whole life. She grew up and married William Macon Crumley. Carrie's father gave them a house as a wedding gift. Carrie and William had three children. We know little else of Carrie's adult life. She died in May 1921 at the age of 66.

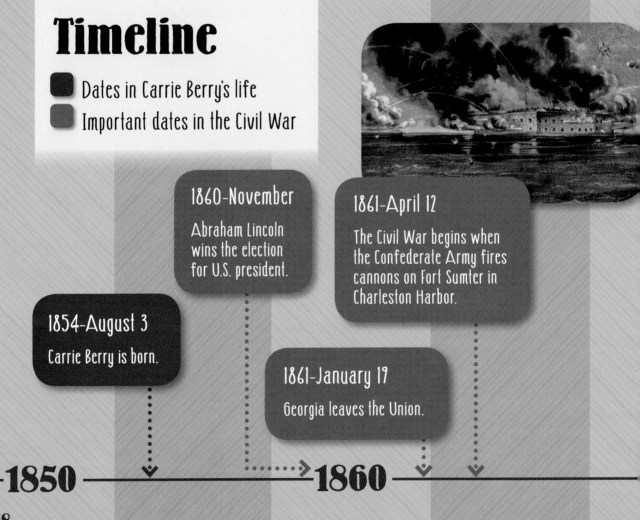

Timeline

■ Dates in Carrie Berry's life
■ Important dates in the Civil War

1860-November

Abraham Lincoln wins the election for U.S. president.

1861-April 12

The Civil War begins when the Confederate Army fires cannons on Fort Sumter in Charleston Harbor.

1854-August 3

Carrie Berry is born.

1861-January 19

Georgia leaves the Union.

1850   1860

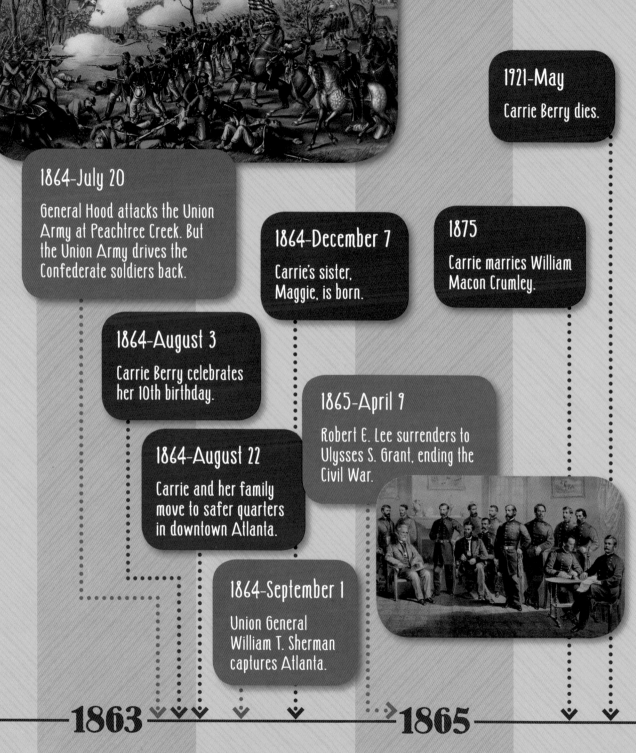

1921-May

Carrie Berry dies.

1864-July 20

General Hood attacks the Union Army at Peachtree Creek. But the Union Army drives the Confederate soldiers back.

1864-December 7

Carrie's sister, Maggie, is born.

1875

Carrie marries William Macon Crumley.

1864-August 3

Carrie Berry celebrates her 10th birthday.

1865-April 9

Robert E. Lee surrenders to Ulysses S. Grant, ending the Civil War.

1864-August 22

Carrie and her family move to safer quarters in downtown Atlanta.

1864-September 1

Union General William T. Sherman captures Atlanta.

1863

1865

Glossary

ammunition (am-yuh-NISH-uhn)—bullets and other objects that can be fired from weapons

blockade (blok-ADE)—a closing off of an area to keep people or supplies from going in or out

commence (kuh-MENSS)—to begin or start

corpse (KORPS)—a dead body

earnest (UR-nist)—serious

evacuate (ee-VAK-yoo-ate)—to leave an area during a time of danger

fret (FRET)—to worry constantly

oblige (uh-BLIJE)—to feel forced to do something

plantation (plan-TAY-shuhn)—a large farm where crops such as cotton and sugarcane are grown; before 1865 plantations were run by slave labor

regulate (reg-yuh-LAYT)—to arrange or order

territory (TER-uh-tor-ee)—an area under the control of a country

torment (tor-MENT)—to cause pain and suffering

trim (TRIM)—decorate

worsted (WURST-ud)—a smooth type of yarn

Read More

Baxter, Roberta. *The Southern Home Front of the Civil War.* Why We Fought: The Civil War. Chicago: Heinemann Library, 2011.

Fein, Eric. *Weapons, Gear, and Uniforms of the Civil War.* Equipped for Battle. North Mankato, Minn.: Capstone Press, 2012.

Ford, Carin T. *An Overview of the American Civil War Through Primary Sources.* The Civil War Through Primary Sources. Berkeley Heights, N.J.: Enslow, 2013.

Critical Thinking Using the Common Core

1. Until the spring of 1864, Carrie Berry's life was like that of most children. Discuss the ways in which daily life changed after General Sherman invaded her city. (Key Ideas and Details)

2. Returning Atlanta citizens blamed those who had stayed behind for not stopping the destruction of their city. Do you think they were right or wrong to do so? Support your answer. (Key Ideas and Details)

3. Carrie Berry wrote about Civil War battles fought in her hometown. Write about a current news event that either is having an effect on your daily life now, or could in the future. (Integration of Knowledge and Ideas)

Internet Sites

FactHound offers a safe, fun way to find Internet sites related to this book. All of the sites on FactHound have been researched by our staff.

Here's all you do:

Visit www.facthound.com

Type in this code: 9781476541921

 Check out projects, games and lots more at **www.capstonekids.com**

Index